TALKING ABOUT DIVORCE

EARL A. GROLLMAN

A Dialogue Between Parent and Child

Illustrations by Alison Cann

BEACON PRESS / BOSTON

Copyright©1975 by Earl A. Grollman

Illustrations copyright ©1975 by Alison Cann

Beacon Press books are published under the auspices
of the Unitarian Universalist Association

Published simultaneously in hardcover and paperback editions

Simultaneous publication in Canada by Saunders of Toronto, Ltd.

All rights reserved

Printed in the United States of America

9 8 7 6 5 4 3 2 1

I would like to express my gratitude to Gobin Stair and Dick Bartlett for their invaluable assistance in preparing this book.

Library of Congress Cataloging in Publication Date

Grollman, Earl A
  Talking about divorce.
  Bibliography: pp. 83-87
  SUMMARY: A guide to helping small children of divorcing parents understand
and accept the fact that their parents are no longer able to live in the same residence
together. Includes a parents' guide, sources for further help, and a bibliography of
fiction and nonfiction about divorce.
  1. Divorce—United States—Juvenile literature.   2. Parent and child.
3. Children of divorced parents—Juvenile literature. [1. Divorce.]
I. Cann, Alison.   II. Title
HQ 834.G76   301.42'84   75-5289
ISBN 0-8070-2374-4
ISBN 0-8070-2375-2 (pbk.)

TO PARENTS

You are now walking down the lonely road of separation and divorce. How will you tell your child that you will no longer live together as a family?

The pages immediately following this preface are written with the hope that you and your youngster will be sympathetically guided toward an honest understanding of the meaning of divorce.

Before you begin the family dialogue, first read the Parents' Guide beginning on page 55. You will obtain the best results when you have carefully decided what material in the children's text should be stressed— and how it can best be presented to your child.

Success will not depend solely on the spoken word. It is you who must make the child believe that you are still vitally concerned about his or her future. The child should sense that you are not only an understanding reader, but also a caring listener.

Even though you and your spouse will walk in separate paths, the challenging task is to demonstrate to your youngsters both by word and by touch that you remain parents and will love them always.

Earl A. Grollman

You know
Mommy and
Daddy
have not
been
getting
along,

don't
you?

How many
times have you
heard us
arguing ?

Now everyone
arques
from time to time.

Just like you
and your
friends.

People have differences.

It is natural to be **angry** sometimes. It is not always wrong to RAISE your VOICE

and
LOSE
YOUR
TeMPer.

But for us, your parents, we do not just have a little fight. We seem to be

arguing all the time.

You can tell by the
way we are picking
on each other

You
see
Mommy
crying
sometimes.

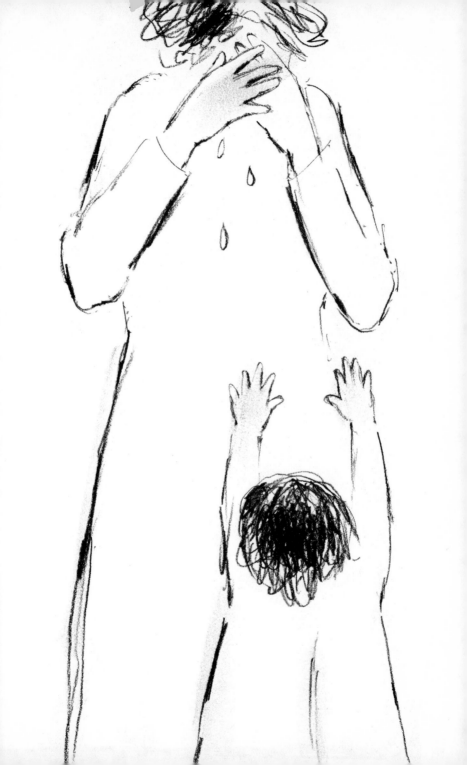

You know Daddy
is not home
like he
used to be.

Sometimes he leaves
right after a quarrel.

Have you
noticed this?

17

The
reason
is
because
Mommy
and
Daddy
are no
longer
happy with
each other.

That's
why we
are
sad.

And not only
are we MEAN
to one another,
sometimes we
Yell

AT YOU
for no good
reason,
even when
it isn't
your fault.

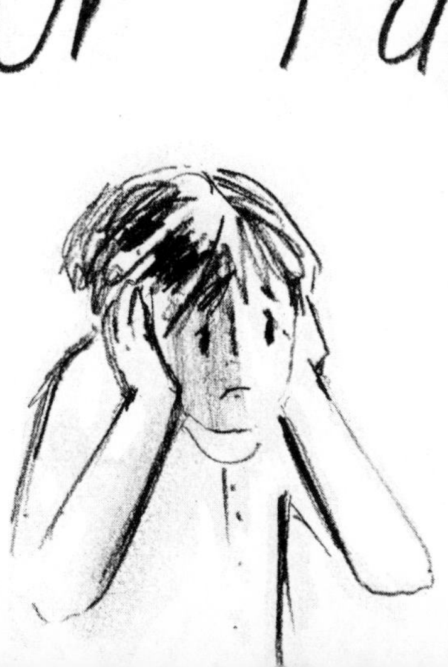

It's like when you don't get a good night's sleep-

The next day
aren't you grumpy?

You just don't
feel right.

That's the way
it is with Mommy
and Daddy.
We aren't happy with
each other. We
don't want to
live together.

I know it hurts you
to hear this.

You've
watched us.

You've seen how we are, haven't you?

This is why we decided not to stay together anymore.

This is called
DIVORCE
It is when
Mommy and
Daddy will no
longer live in
the same house
together.

Why are we
doing this? It is not
because you have
done anything wrong.

You are **NOT** the
reason for us wanting
to live away from
each other.

DO you understand?

You bring us
happiness
even when many
things in our
marriage
are wrong.

You are the
Wonderful
part of our
life.

You are **NOT**
to blame for the
divorce.

You are **NOT**
to **blame**.

Mommy and
Daddy are not
    perfect
We've both made
mistakes.

We are sorry
about the divorce.
More than you
    know.

We
know how
unhappy
you are.

Tell us how
you **really** feel.

We will listen.

we
want
to
know.

When
something sad
happens, people
do many things
Some want to

Scream

at the top of
their lungs.

And

some

just

want

to be

alone.

Are you
frightened ?

Are you
angry ?

It is **all right** to
let go of some of
your feelings.
You may feel
better if you do.

But no matter
what you do
   Mommy and Daddy
will no longer live
         together.

We thought
about it for a
long, long time.

Our decision
is final.

Our marriage is not a good one.

It is a mistake.

Sometimes the way to correct a mistake is to make a change.

And the way
we will change is by
living

apart.

Even though
we will no longer
be husband and wife,
we will still

be your

Mommy

and

Daddy.

We are your parents. We will take care of you the best way we know how.

That is
the one
thing
both of us
agree on.

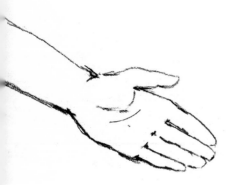

You are
our child
and
we will
LOVE
YOU always.

A PARENTS' GUIDE TO *TALKING ABOUT DIVORCE*

INTRODUCTION

Marriage has been described as the one enterprise which we expect 93 percent of people to enter and 100 percent to be successful.

Not all marriages are successful. Perhaps this is why you are now reading this book. You are contemplating divorce. You are justifiably concerned and apprehensive. To you it means an end to your cherished hopes and dreams. To your child it could seem like the end of the world. How are you going to face the turbulence of this frightening experience? Is there a good way to break the news to the youngster?

Most of the volumes written for children of divorce have been narratives about a mythical Dick and Jane—stories about fictional characters, novel descriptions of *other* children.

Talking About Divorce: A Dialogue Between Parent and Child is about real people, namely you, the readers. You are about to tell your child how your divorce will touch and change your customary family living. You will tell the youngster just what the divorce will mean in terms of his or her future. Equally important in the dialogue is your encouragement to your child—your willingness to share your child's real feelings, whether it be anger, resentment, hostility or just plain relief that an unhappy family is breaking up. Whatever your child's emotions at this critical time, you all must now try to communicate the best way you know how.

While insight is a gift, you, the parents, must now place yourselves in a position to receive it. You should prepare yourselves for it. Observe your children and hear the tone and timbre of their voices. Let the youngsters tell you how they feel, what they think, what they wish to know.

In order to prepare yourself for this dialogue, first absorb the contents of the children's read-along section. Then read and reread this guide. Determine in advance the best method of interpreting the material to your child: what points to emphasize, what lessons to underscore. Anticipate problems not discussed in these pages. Where will your child now live? With whom? What about visitations? Even if the details of your divorce are not complete, let your child know that you are working out the arrangements and will always keep him or her informed of developments.

In your discussion, honesty is the *only* policy. One of the worst problems for the child is lack of understanding because of parental secrecy. Once the matter is out in the open, it can be faced, for then it is not quite so frightening. You only hurt your child when you deny him or her the opportunity of facing a painful but necessary reality of life. The worst actuality is often preferable to uncertainty.

Difficult as it may be, this book should, if possible, be read with both parents present. This would serve many purposes. It lessens the possibility of one partner's making the other the culprit. In a united explanation you indicate an attempt to work for the best welfare of your child. This means not letting your youngster become a weapon in the battle between the parents or asking the child to take sides. It connotes a *shared* interest. Obviously, in some circumstances, both parents cannot be present for the family dialogue. One can only do one's best under existing circumstances.

The conversation should not take place after husband and wife have been arguing. Too often in an atmosphere of heated anger, the hysterical parents rush headlong to the youngster with "We can't stand it any longer longer! We're getting divorced!" Separation and its meaning should be approached gently and sympathetically during a time of relative relaxation and tranquillity. Make sure the house is quiet and you have ample time to be alone with the family.

This book is not designed to be read in one sitting. Many children are not able to absorb this information quickly.

Try to answer questions with the most appropriate factual responses. Speak *with* the youngster, not *at* him. All children need to talk, not just to be talked to. Converse in such a way as to encourage the ability—both your child's and yours—to think, digest, and understand what is significant in what each says.

Try to discern the child's real concerns. The deeper problem may not appear at first. Each of us, whether child or adult, lives in a different perceptual world; we see and construct our pictures of the universe in terms of our own needs and emotional experiences. We must realize that each person has his own, unique way of viewing, of framing a view of the world around him.

One of the great rights you can give your child at this time is the right to feel. Never turn away from his or her thoughts or brand them as "insignificant" or "childish." Allow resentment and guilt to wither in the sunlight rather than attempt to pull them out by the roots by condemning your child for genuine emotions.

The youngster may ask you to repeat the explanation. Even adults who hear of a crisis may say, "I don't believe it. It can't be true." So, gently, say it again. The child's need of repeated explanation is his way of coping with and working through the perplexing situation.

What is said is important, but how it is said has even greater bearing on whether the child will develop neurotic anxiety or accept, within his capacity, the fact of separation. The best explanation is often nonverbal. If you hold the youngster close to you, he will feel your warmth and really know that he is not being abandoned.

Equally important, you as parents must realize that your divorce does not mean you have forsaken your child. Know that a youngster is better off in a broken home than an unhappy one. A marriage that is doggedly maintained "for the sake of the children" could create more severe problems, not only for you but, through you, for the youngster. A child living with disturbed parents more often gets into psychiatric difficulty than one whose parents have been strong and mature enough to sever their unfortunate relationship.

Even with new problems you are not alone: Read carefully the section *For Further Help* (page 75) to determine the services which can best assist you and your children. And finally, the section *For Further Reading* (page 83), will enable you to engage in an even more insightful family dialogue about divorce.

"You know Mommy and Daddy have not been getting along, don't you?"

Divorce is the honest admission that husband and wife are not happy with each other and no longer wish to live together. There is no reason to pretend otherwise. Initially, it seems easier to respond to the agony of breakup with untruths. But if you expect your child to be honest with you, you must be honest with him or her. Ultimately, lying leads to confusion, misconception and distrust. Evasions indicate your own inability to handle this stressful situation.

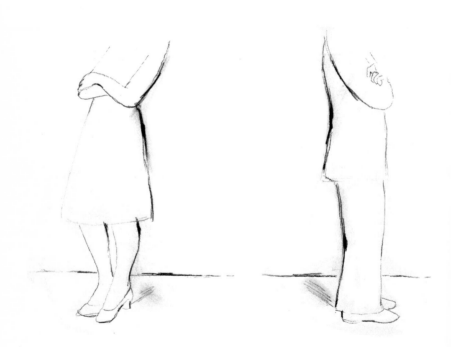

"People have differences. . . . It is natural to be angry sometimes."

Language has a different meaning for parents and children. The youngster hears the words "anger," "raising your voice," "losing your temper," and in the future could associate these phrases with painful separation. Let him or her know that it is only natural to have arguments. One is not bad because of angry thoughts and feelings. But make the distinction between the playmates' infrequent squabbles and the parents' constant, intense disputes.

"You see Mommy crying sometimes. . . . Daddy is not home like he used to be. . . . Sometimes we yell at you for no good reason."

It is futile to believe that your prolonged upheaval has remained a secret. Even the very young person senses frightening changes taking place. When there is tension, the child experiences depression around him. Very often, he or she perceives the inevitability of divorce even before the parents have reached this conclusion.

"You are not the reason for us wanting to live away from each other. . . . You are not to blame for the divorce. . . . Do you think you are?"

The child may believe that he must be responsible for the separation. After all, in his limited experience, unfortunate things happen when he is naughty. So he searches for the terrible act that caused the breakup. To him, divorce must be some punishment for wrongdoing. An unreasoning guilt drives him into self-pity and even self-punishment.

Say again and again that you are unhappy with each other but not with him. The reason for the divorce is not because the child was bad. As long as he believes that he has caused the separation, he can conjure up the illusion that he has the power to bring you all back together again.

"Mommy and Daddy are not perfect. We both made mistakes."

A youngster often believes that the divorce must be his or her fault. Many children think parents are perfect. Therefore, the fault must lie with the child.

It is important for the child to realize that adults are not all-powerful and all-knowing. You demonstrate the highest maturity when you acknowledge that you make mistakes. It is the reward and penalty of being human not only to err but to admit weaknesses.

*"Tell us how you really feel. We will listen. . . . It is all right
to let go of some of your feelings. You may feel better if
you do."*

A child's emotional response is a complicated mechanism. He is
distressed that one parent will now leave the household. The familiar
design of family life is disrupted. The youngster may even believe that
he was magically selected for personal pain and punishment.

How the child reacts depends on many factors: age, custody arrangements, coping mechanisms, previous relationship with parents. Each
child experiences the conflict in a different way, for each child's response is unique. If the parents do not tell the truth and the child is not
permitted to express his feelings, the following are some of the symptoms
divorce could provoke:

Denial and Silence

The young employ the mechanism of denial to protect the ego from disagreeable circumstances. The reaction to the trauma of divorce might be, "I don't believe it. My parents are just having another argument. They would never leave me." The ability to deny unpleasant parts of reality is the counterpart of an hallucinatory wish fulfillment. In a sense, it amounts to closing one's eyes to the real state of affairs.

Older youth, also, may not tell the truth about family situations. Studies reveal that many students often lie about their family after their parents are divorced and talk as if their mother and father were still living together.

Regression

Following the traumatic experience of divorce, the youngster might retreat to earlier stages of development. He could return to infantile tendencies belonging to the period preceding the conflict. Regression is the result of failure to master new anxiety. He is just afraid to take the next step and may feel more secure when he retraces his steps back to the time of safety before the breakup. In a primitive return to earlier forms of gratification, speech often becomes babyish. Or he may suck his thumb, wet the bed, and whine a great deal to demand attention. It's like saying, "I'm just a little baby again. Don't leave me. Stay together!"

Bodily Distress

Psychological anxiety is sometimes accompanied by physiological change: trembling, restlessness, loss of appetite, an increase in pulse and respiration rates, nausea, diarrhea, urinary frequency, and fitful sleep which may be interrupted by frightening dreams. Sometimes these dreams become so threatening that the child believes himself in danger. No longer is he sure that food, shelter, and comfort will be forthcoming. His reactions may also be an unconscious method of trying to unite the parents to take care of the now-sick child.

Hostility

The child is threatened with separation and loss of love. He wants revenge. When enraged, the first impulse is to strike the person or persons who caused so much pain. (Some parents may not like hostility in themselves but just will not tolerate it in their children.)

The youngster may interpret the breakup of the home as a form of abandonment. He feels that he has been betrayed by those he loves best and needs most. He wishes to retaliate by getting even. He may become so furious that he attempts to destroy everything around him, and eventually himself.

Some parents unwisely react to this anger by threats of further punishment. But the young person has had enough abuse. Let him know that you understand feelings of resentment. Listen to him if he tells you about his. Encourage him to express his feelings and answer his questions frankly and lovingly.

Crying

Crying is a natural expression. The child is anxious and guilty—anxious because his future is being threatened, guilty because of an actual or imagined role in the domestic strife. He may cry as he expresses this painful emotion. When his tears flow, he feels better. He experiences pain but does not know how to verbalize it. Tears make up for words.

The worst possible response is for the youngster to repress his feelings. An individual who stoically keeps his grief bottled up inside may later find release in a more serious psychological explosion.

Be realistic enough to say, "I know you are crying because you care so much. You feel strongly because you love us and are afraid." In this way you allow him or her the opportunity of relieving tension. Otherwise the adult deprives the child of giving expression to the true emotion of the sadness of separation.

"Our decision is final."

In a desire to appease the youngster, some adults attempt to soften the blow by saying, "Maybe we will think it over again." So the hope against hope that perhaps his parents will not be divorced is allowed to remain. Once again, when the decision is irrevocable, honesty is the *only* formula. Things cannot be changed; the parents will not be re-united. Help the child to deal with life's realities. The truth is that the separation is unalterable.

"Sometimes the way to correct a mistake is to make a change. And the way we will change is by living apart."

Life's challenges are the personal choices available to all of us. One profits from yesterday's experiences by learning to pursue new meanings for tomorrow.

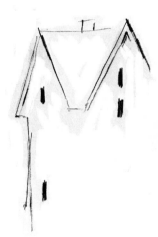

"We are your parents. . . . and we will love you always."

The child of divorce still has two parents. You are both alive and well and care deeply about your child. After the separation, he or she may even be surprised to discover that the house is happily quiet for the first time. The youngster can perhaps spend more creative time with his parents than ever before. Now that the tumult and the shouting have disappeared, the individual parent and child may be more able to rediscover one another. Distance does not have to diminish love.

SOME FINAL THOUGHTS

Some parents try to make up for their absence or compensate for their guilt by giving their children everything they want. Every trivial demand becomes a compelling command. A steady flow of expensive but unnecessary gifts pours in. In addition, the parents continue to spoil the child by doing only "fun things" and failing to discipline the child when necessary. They try to buy affection by being the "good guys." They do not understand that love cannot be purchased.

Don't try to "make up" by overindulgence. A child needs to bend efforts toward achievement, but overindulgence deprives the youngster of attaining satisfactions by his own efforts. Nor should he or she be subject to the parents' recurring personal hostility. The child should never be treated as an unwanted burden, a perpetual source of trouble. Let the youngster receive the privilege of growing up—occasionally being naughty and mischievous. Parents should be neither too demanding nor too permissive. The goal is balance—something never easy for parents under any circumstances.

Divorced parents should avoid the temptation of making the child a substitute adult or surrogate partner. A youngster does not replace the absent mate. Physical intimacy such as sharing a bedroom should be tactfully avoided. Seductive and sexually stimulating situations cause embarrassment and guilt. Your child is not your lover-companion-confessor-spouse. He should be accepted within the limits of his psychological and intellectual capabilities. He is still a child.

Often one mate will blame the other entirely for the trouble in the marriage. When one parent is disparaged, the child is forced into a painful choice, having to take sides. In the bitter contest for the child's affection and the parent's exoneration, such statements are frequently heard: "Your father never cared for you" or, "Your mother is selfish and only thinks about herself." The child is "used" in this vendetta as a means for transmitting adult contempt and retribution. The result is the youngster's further insecurity. After all, no one likes to think that his father is completely unfeeling; no one wants a self-indulgent mother. The youngster may feel that it is hopeless to even try to be good, that this is his psychological inheritance—doomed to be bad, just like his parents.

The child needs to feel wanted and loved, by two parents who are neither saints nor villains. He experiences an intolerable hurt when his mother and father say anything denigrating about the other. Is there any reason to blacken each other's character and then ask the youngster to judge between weaknesses? Such a feud only keeps alive bitterness and misunderstanding. If you need revenge, you are not completely free from your former mate.

On the other hand, don't go overboard in the opposite direction. You do not have to stress the other's virtues. The child perceives duplicity and loses faith in the parent who tells him what he knows to be false. He thinks, "If he [or she] was so wonderful, why are they getting divorced?"

Nor do you need to go into minute detail about all the reasons for divorce. Remember, you are speaking to a child, not your therapist. It is neither necessary nor wise to isolate single issues. In an effort for honesty, one mother tried to explain the motive for divorce by saying, "We just can't agree on money. I want to buy clothes and Daddy won't let me." Now financial difficulties were one of the causes for the division between this husband and wife. By trying to be specific, however, the mother oversimplified the problem and the child responded, "I'll tell you what. Keep my allowance. I won't buy any candy. This way we can all stay together." Events described individually seem trivial and surmountable. The single conflict is only a symptom of the over-all, complex source of disharmony. You might instead say, "You have watched us for so long and you have seen us unhappy for so many reasons."

What if the mate runs off and shows no interest in the child? The other parent should acknowledge this reality and help the youngster come to grips with it. Even under these circumstances however, it is not necessary to portray the other party as a completely wicked individual. Did you not marry him or her for his or her good points? What were they? Let the child respect traits that deserve praise and genuinely acknowledge faults. In short, do not paint a false picture of either the other's perfections or shortcomings. Try to place the love for your child above your resentment for your mate. The truth is that both parents are human.

For both adults and child, being human means living with problems. There are times when even the best-informed and well-intentioned are simply inadequate. Seeking help from a therapist, psychiatrist, psychologist, or a child-guidance clinic is not an admission of weakness, but a demonstration of real love and strength. (*See* For Further Help)

Some danger signals that indicate that professional assistance should be considered include: delinquency, unwillingness to remain in school, difficulties in learning, sexual perversion, obsessive-compulsive reactions, tics, as well as withdrawal and friendlessness.

This is a time of stress and strain and your discussions with a sympathetic but objective professional may help not only your youngster but yourself as well.

It is important for you as parents to recognize your own anxieties. Regardless of what you say, your emotional feelings are transmitted to your child. Your capacity for empathy with the child can be blocked by your own personal distress at the time of separation.

You will get discouraged. At best, it is not easy to raise youngsters. Remember—everyone gets depressed during difficult periods of transition. Just as you don't demand too much from the youngster, so you should not create unrealistic requirements for yourself. Goals must be flexible. Take one day at a time. Accept what little you can do at the moment, even as you strive to accomplish a little more in the future. If you reject yourself as a failure, you will only create a more difficult environment for yourself and your child.

You can only bring alive an outlook that is authentic for you. The actual words you use are less important than the attitude you convey. It is only as you now search and find answers for yourself that you will help your child to search and find answers for himself or herself. This will demand your best wisdom, your most creative efforts. For the real challenge is not just how to explain divorce to your child but how to make peace with it yourself.

FOR FURTHER HELP

Child Guidance and Family Associations

Child-guidance clinics are located in most cities in the United States. Consult your telephone directory or:

National Association for Mental Health
1800 North Kent Street
Rosslyn Station
Arlington, Va. 22209

For family agencies with comprehensive casework services, write:

Family Service Association of America
44 East 23rd Street
New York, N. Y. 10010

A valuable directory with a complete listing of all mental-health facilities in the U.S. may be purchased for a small fee. The Mental Health Directory can be obtained from:

National Clearinghouse for Mental Health
5454 Wisconsin Avenue
Chevy Chase, Md. 20015

For an entire list of resource groups, services, and counseling programs in your area write:

Catalyst
6 East 82nd Street
New York, N. Y. 10028

Also check with your local YMCA, university, college, or yellow pages for counseling services. Before you make a selection, investigate all the services in your area and request a preliminary consultation.

Clergy and Religious Agencies

Your minister may be of help during your personal difficulty. He or she represents a concerned religious community offering spiritual insights into inner conflicts. Not all pastors, however, are sufficiently educated and trained for crisis intervention. For further information regarding clergy with accredited counseling skills contact:

> The American Association of Pastoral Counselors
> 3 West 29th Street
> New York, N.Y. 10001

The following religious organizations and agencies may also be of assistance:

Protestant:	Joint Department of Family Life
	National Council of the Churches of Christ
	475 Riverside Drive
	New York, N.Y. 10027
Catholic:	National Conference of Catholic Charities
	1346 Connecticut Avenue
	Washington, D.C. 20036
Jewish:	Council of Jewish Federations and Welfare Funds
	315 Park Avenue South
	New York, N.Y. 10010

Court Counseling Services

A most promising approach to the problems people face in divorce is found in the family court. The name of the service may be called "conciliation counselor," "friend of the court," or "family counseling agency of the probate court." The emphasis is upon understanding and assistance rather than punishment.

The most notable of the court counseling services is that of Judge Paul W. Alexander in Toledo, Ohio. His Family Court Center provides customary legal aid along with services from psychiatrists, marriage counselors, pediatricians, and nurses.

The components vary from court to court but often include such services as counseling, referral to community agencies, program development to assist in coping with domestic conflicts and restructuring family lives, investigation into matters of custody, and mediation of visitation rights.

For further details contact your family or probate court or the professional organization of state and local conciliation courts:

Conference of Conciliation Courts
Room 241
111 N. Hill Street
Los Angeles, Calif. 90012

Divorce Reform

The great majority of the thousands of divorce cases heard each week are granted. Unfortunately, in many proceedings fabrication, collusion, and fraud abound. Perjury has too often become the rule in many divorce courts.

There are many people working on divorce reform—attempting to make the laws more honest and more equitable.

Among the divorce-reform organizations are:

Divorce Reform, Inc.
735 N. Snelling Avenue
St. Paul, Minn. 55104

Men's Liberation, Inc.
153 E. 18th Street
New York, N.Y. 10003

Minnesota Divorce Justice League
761 Raymond Avenue
St. Paul, Minn. 55114

National Conference of Commissioners on Uniform State Laws
1155 E. 60th Street
Chicago, Ill. 60637
(One of the oldest organizations, established in 1892 to work toward divorce reform).

National Council on Family Relations
Task Force on Divorce and Divorce Reform
701 N. Pegram Street
Alexandria, Va. 22304

NOISE (National Organization to Insure Support Enforcement)
10 Columbus Circle
New York, N.Y. 10019

U.S. Divorce Reform, Inc.
P.O. Box 243
Kenwood, Calif. 95452

Women's Equity Action League
National Press Building
529 14th Street, N.W.
Committee on Divorce
Room 538
Washington, D.C. 20004

Lawyers

Laws regarding divorce and custody differ from state to state. Make sure your lawyer is both experienced and trustworthy. A tax attorney may know little about the intricacies of divorce. *Please note:* it is unconscionable for parents to involve their child in the legal procedure of divorce.

If you have any questions, call your local bar association, legal aid society, lawyers' referral service, or:

American Bar Association
1155 East 60th Street
Chicago, Ill. 60637

Family Law Section
American Bar Association
Milwaukee County Courthouse
901 N. 9th Street
Milwaukee, Wis. 53233
(Committees on divorce laws, alimony, custody, interstate and international support, marriage law, and family counseling.)

Women's Law Center
351 Broadway
New York, N.Y. 10013
(Assists women with legal problems of divorce.)

Marriage and Family Counselors

The profession of marriage counselor is a comparatively new one but marriage counselors have proved to be extremely helpful for short-range supportive therapy. Unfortunately, exacting standards have not been firmly established for all of those who have assumed this important role.

For details concerning certified marriage counselors and professional services contact:

American Association of Marriage and Family Counselors
225 Yale Avenue
Claremont, Calif. 91711

In many cities there are special counseling services for families dealing with divorce such as:

California Divorce Council
2241 South Atlantic Boulevard, Suite G
Monterey Park, Calif. 91754

Divorce Consultants, Associated
2509 Nevada Avenue, S.
St. Louis Park, Minn. 55426

Divorce Counseling Service
3215 Columbia Pike
Arlington, Va. 22204

Organizations

There are a variety of self-help groups and organizations devoted to helping families of divorce.

The largest international, nonprofit, nonsectarian organization, with a membership of 80,000 in over 600 chapters, concerned with the welfare of single parents and their children is:

Parents Without Partners, Incorporated
7910 Woodmont Avenue
Washington, D.C. 20014

A strong supportive women's organization that often offers divorce-lawyer referral and consciousness-raising sessions for mutual problems is:

NOW (National Organization for Women)
National Task Force, Marriage and Divorce
7 Hill Road
Greenwich, Conn. 06830

or

NOW
1957 East 73rd Street
Chicago, Ill. 60649

There might be special problems because of religious affiliation. For separated and divorced Catholics, there are more than 35 chapters offering educational, social, and counseling services. Write:

Divorced Catholic Group
c/o Paulist Center
5 Park Street
Boston, Mass. 02108

Many church organizations offer help to families of divorce. One such group, created by the Presbyterian Church to provide an environment of empathy and understanding, is:

Divorce Lifeline
1013 Eighth Avenue
Seattle, Wash. 98104

Based in California but with chapters throughout the country the Momma organization is geared for single mothers, serving the practical and emotional needs of raising children alone through cooperative baby-sitting and counseling, medical, and legal referral services.

MOMMA
Box 567
Venice, Calif. 90291

Physicians

The family physician is often a valuable resource in understanding and assisting the parent and child of divorce. The family doctor knows the patient through years of personal medical service and has a unique opportunity to observe his or her physical and emotional health. The compassionate insights of the family doctor are just as important, perhaps more important, than the medicines he prescribes.

For information, write:

American Academy of Family Physicians
1740 West 92nd Street
Kansas City, Mo. 64114

    or

The American Medical Association
535 North Dearborn Street
Chicago, Ill. 60610

Psychological and Psychiatric Service

Psychological and psychiatric counseling is a learned art in which a highly trained person with acquired basic knowledge and skills helps divorced families.

The following is a partial list of psychological and psychiatric associations with accredited professionals and services:

Psychological: American Psychological Association
1200 17th Street, N.W.
Washington, D.C. 20036

Psychiatric: American Psychiatric Association
1700 18th Street, N.W.
Washington, D.C. 20009

American Psychoanalytic Association
1 East 57th Street
New York, N.Y. 10022

Social Workers

Trained social workers have come into their own as counselors for people in crisis. Many work within the context of mental-hygiene agencies, child-guidance clinics, and comprehensive mental-health centers.

For further details concerning social workers and their respective agencies, contact:

National Association of Social Workers
1425 H Street, N.W.
Washington, D.C. 20005

or

Office of Child Development
Office of the Secretary
Department of Health, Education, and Welfare
P.O. Box 1182
Washington, D. C. 20013

United Way

The Information and Referral Service

Alphabetically, United Way is the last in this listing of where to go for help. Practically, their Information and Referral Service may be the first to call.

The service provides information on and referral to community resources for the most expedient handling of the problem of divorce.

The service is especially helpful because many in crisis cannot identify their source of stress or judge what helping organization might be most beneficial. The Information and Referral Service of the United Way is able to assess the applicant's needs and make a determination about an appropriate agency in the area. It could be a legal-aid society, a family-service association, a children's camp, a big-brothers' or sisters' organization, a mental-health facility, a day-care center, a housing authority, a child-guidance clinic, or a social service.

Where to go for help? Take time to investigate all the possibilities. The choice may be one of the most important decisions of your life.

FOR FURTHER READING

Suggested Fiction About Divorce

WRITTEN FOR CHILDREN

Chronologically by age

Goff, Beth, *Where Is Daddy?* (Boston: Beacon Press, 1969).
Ages 3-6.
This slim volume tells the story of what happens to a little girl whose parents become divorced. Even though she is initially confused and frightened, she is later able to make a suitable adjustment.

Lexeau, Joan M., *Me Day* (New York: Dial Press, 1971).
Ages 4-7.
One of the very few books to deal with divorce in a black family. A tender narrative of a boy's fantasy involving the return of his absent father on "me day," a very special occasion.

Kindred, Wendy, *Lucky Wilma* (New York: Dial Press, 1973).
Ages 4-8.
Not all divorces are sad. Wilma looks forward to each Saturday when she and her daddy will be together. She even helps her father to discover new meanings for himself in life.

Adams, Florence, *Mushy Eggs* (New York: G.P. Putman's Sons, 1973).
Ages 7-10.
How do youngsters react to a fatherless family? It is interesting to note that one child says "we" are divorced. Not only is the mother separated from her husband but the child also feels divorced from his father. The narrative is powerful but not mushy.

Mann, Peggy, *My Dad Lives in a Downtown Hotel* (Garden City, New York: Doubleday, 1973).
Ages 8-10.
A first person account of a boy's innermost feelings during divorce. The ending is hopeful. He finally realizes that he is not the cause of the separation and that his parents still love him.

Blue, Rose, *A Month of Sundays* (New York: Franklin Watts, 1972).
Ages 9-11.
A believable tale of how divorce changes the life of a boy: a different environment, a tired mother, and a father who visits only on Sundays.

Blume, Judy, *It's Not the End of the World* (New York: Bradbury Press, 1972).
Ages 9-12.

The sensitive emotions of a twelve year old girl who keeps hoping that her troubled parents become reconciled. Ultimately, she accepts both her parents and the reality of the divorce.

Klein, Norma, *Taking Sides* (New York: Pantheon Books, 1974).
Ages 10-12.

Written from the perspective of a girl who lives with her divorced father and sees her mother only on weekends. She displays amazing insights into her parents' delicate problems and at times seems more mature than the adults.

Mazer, Harry, *Guy Lenny* (New York: Delacort Press, 1971).
Ages 10-12.

The tough dilemma of a twelve-year-old boy who becomes the focal point of a bitter custody battle.

Stolz, Mary, *Leap Before You Look* (New York: Harper and Row, 1973).
Ages 12-16.

An honest account of a girl's realization of her parents' marital difficulties and her inability to accept the impending divorce.

Non-fiction:

Gardner, Richard A, *The Boys' and Girls' Book About Divorce* (Scranton, Pennsylvania: Science House, Inc., 1970).
Ages 13-17.

A child psychiatrist addresses himself to the myriad emotional problems that beset children of divorce: who's to blame, anger and its uses, the fear of being alone, and how to get along with parents who are living apart.

Suggested Books About Divorce and Children

WRITTEN FOR ADULTS

Despert, J. Louise, *Children of Divorce* (Garden City, New York: Doubleday, 1953).

One of the pioneering efforts and yet contemporary. In a straightforward, conversational style, an in-depth discussion of the emotional problems of parents and children, suggesting creative ways of meeting the difficulties of divorce.

Goldstein, Joseph, Anna Freud, and Albert J. Solnit, *Beyond the Best Interests of the Child* (New York: Free Press, 1973).

A provocative application of psychoanalytic insight to child custody law by professors of law, psychiatry, and child study. The volume concludes that the parent who wins custody of the child should make all decisions about the youngster's life including when or whether the other parent should visit. It recommends that two equally acceptable parents draw lots for custody. These and other controversial views contribute to formulating a new code that will go "beyond the best interests of the child."

Grollman, Earl A., ed., *Explaining Divorce to Children* (Boston: Beacon Press, 1967).
   Nine experts view the effects of divorce from the perspective of psychiatry, sociology, law, child psychology, and the three major religions. The contributors point the way for parents to deal realistically and reassuringly with their children and thereby relieve the strain on both the children and themselves.

Hallet, Kathryn, *A Guide for Single Parents* (Millbrae, California: Celestial Arts, 1974).
   A useful and effective approach using transactional analysis to help children of divorce and single parents. There is a suggested divorce ritual in which parents return their wedding rings and promise to respect each other as well as continue to care, support, and love their children.

Simon, Anne W., *Stepchild in the Family: A View of Children in Remarriage* (New York: The Odyssey Press, 1964).
   What happens to the seven million stepchildren in the United States, the result of the unprecedented rise in remarriage? This psychological and social study competently examines the unexplored area of step families.

Steinzor, Bernard, *When Parents Divorce* (New York: Pantheon Books, 1969).
   Out of an unhappy marriage a healthy divorce can emerge. Practical information is offered in dealing with children: their divided loyalties, which parent is better suited to have custody, visitation rights, over-intense attachment between mother and child, and parental dating.

Stuart, Irving R., and Lawrence E. Abt, *Children of Separation and Divorce* (New York: Grossman Publishers, 1972).
   A collection of articles written by specialists—psychologists, lawyers, clergy, and social workers—that examines the problems confronting children of separation and divorce and suggests how the effects may be minimized or overcome.

Suggested Books About Divorce in General

Bohannan, Paul, ed., *Divorce and After* (Garden City, New York: Doubleday, 1971).
   Though primarily written for professionals, these eleven studies by nine contributors contain provocative sociological material on divorce and its aftermath.

Donelson, Kenneth, and Irene Donelson, *Married Today, Single Tomorrow: Marriage Breakup and the Law* (Garden City, New York: Doubleday, 1969).
   This volume is especially useful for its expert financial and legal counsel. There is also sound advice for divided parenthood and those left alone with the care of the children.

Epstein, Joseph, *Divorced in America: An Anatomy of Loneliness* (New York: E.P. Dutton, 1974).

Intertwined with the social and moral history of divorce is the emotional journey of the author through the dissolution of his own marriage. Chapter VII, *"For the Sake of the Children,"* is very practical.

Goode, William J., *After Divorce* (Glencoe, Illinois: Free Press, 1956).

A systematic study of the post-divorce experiences of urban mothers in Detroit.

Haussamen, Florence, and Mary A. Guitar, *The Divorce Handbook* (New York: Putnam, 1960).

The inexperienced divorce seeker has much to gain by reading about the social, financial, and emotional ramifications of divorce. The chapter entitled *"About the Children"* is particularly helpful.

Hunt, Morton M., *The World of the Formerly Married* (New York: McGraw-Hill, 1966).

An intimate tour of the world of the formerly married through the various scenes of marital strife, separation, and divorce. Convincing encouragement is offered that the end of marriage need not be the end of the world.

Krantzler, Mel, *Creative Divorce* (New York: M. Evans and Company, 1973).

People for whom the suffering of divorce is still raw will find help and hope in the author's personal anecdotal case histories. The section on children of divorce gives humane and useful guidance and comfort.

Metz, Charles V., *Divorce and Custody for Men* (Garden City, New York: Doubleday, 1968).

The head of an organization that counsels men with divorce problems offers guidelines for creating more equitable laws.

Mindey, Carol, *The Divorced Mother: A Guide to Readjustment* (New York: McGraw-Hill, 1969).

The writer, now remarried, gives sound instruction to the 250,000 mothers who are divorced each year. She warns of the emotional problems divorced mothers must face in themselves and their children and suggests ways of a more meaningful and constructive life.

Sheresky, Norman, and Marya Mannes, *Uncoupling: The Art of Coming Apart* (New York: The Viking Press, 1972).

A discussion of the social and legal principles operative in divorce proceedings: hiring of lawyers, separation agreements, alimony, and child custody. With less emotionalism and greater objectivity on the part of the parents, the act of divorce could be accomplished with minimum difficulty and maximum compatibility.

Wheeler, Michael, *No-Fault Divorce* (Boston: Beacon Press, 1974).

Since traditional divorce laws do not often reflect the realities of contemporary marriage, new approaches are recommended to make family-dissolution procedures more truthful and humane. Children of divorce might be better protected with legal representation by a court-appointed attorney.